We Share the World

We Share the World

BILL AYRES

RESOURCE *Publications* · Eugene, Oregon

WE SHARE THE WORLD

Resource Publications
An Imprint of Wipf and Stock Publishers
199 W. 8th Ave., Suite 3
Eugene, OR 97401

www.wipfandstock.com

PAPERBACK ISBN: 979-8-3852-4480-5
HARDCOVER ISBN: 979-8-3852-4481-2
EBOOK ISBN: 979-8-3852-4482-9

04/09/25

For Gayle—my wife, my life—for my family, and for all the poets who have helped and inspired me.

CONTENTS

III

ACKNOWLEDGMENTS

"Prattle"—Small Pond
"Three-Legged Dog"—Plainsongs
"Yanked Out of the House. . . ."
And "Black Hat"—Hollins Critic
"Since No Broken Thing. . ."—Antietam Review
"The Seam Where Spirit. . ."—VWC Review
"I Was Told."—Powatan Review
"Where Our Weight. . ."—river city
"Baggage"—Kit Kat Review
"Monkey"—Blackwater Review
"School"—Trinity Review
"Animal Talk" and "A Song Instead. . ."—Sow's Ear
"You Say Distance. . ."
"This One Made of Rubber"
And "Daddy Long Legs"—Commonweal
"I Start My Life. . ."
"We Share the World,"
and "Not What You Dreamed. . . ."
won Poetry Society of Virginia contests.

I

"I know i am solid and sound."

WALT WHITMAN

STARTING HERE

Does it matter
how you believe the world began
and how you were made?

That the earth was shaped from the corpse
of a murdered giant,
the water his blood, his spit, his sweat,
the soil his flesh,
the rocks his bones?

That your ancestors
were children whom the left leg of that behemoth
sired on his right leg?

That your grandfather was shaped
with hammer and pliers and fire?

That your mother was knitted together with needles?

All birth is violent,
as much for the one receiving it
as for the one giving birth.

A seed is torn open from within.

A beak pecks away at a shell
until it breaks into the light.

Sucking air for the first time,
breathing in, you burst open your lungs;
breathing out, you let the world know how it feels.

BIB BOY

The trick of turning my head
to the side
won't stop you
from feeding me applesauce.

Nor can it protect me
from the creamed turnips
you spoon into my mouth.

Against my will
I am ingesting language.

This syllable is your name
or at least what
you want me to call you.

That string of consonants
and vowels
tastes like a question.

This one has the tang of command.

Some words melt in my mouth
and I swallow them.
Others I spit out.

I duck my chin
when I recognize
I can't hold onto my ignorance.

I clinch my jaw
against knowing.

Pretending not to understand
won't work much longer.

Soon I will slip up
and speak.
It is more than I can stomach.

NO ONE LEARNS TO WALK
AND GOES BACK TO CRAWLING

I can't see much from underfoot in the kitchen.
Holding my head up cricks my neck.
To move means rubbing my knees
and my shins and the tops of my feet
raw across boards, tile, carpet.
Grit sticks to my hands and my forearms.
Stirred up dust coats my tongue.
It makes me cough.
No matter how much I fear standing,
how dizzy it makes me,
I will have to risk walking.
For now, I hold a leg of the table
with one hand and pull myself up.
On my toes, I arch my back.
My trembling fingers reach
and nudge the handle
of what must be a spoon.
I'll pull it down.

THE PINK SMELL OF ERASURE

Didn't you sit beside me in fourth grade,
or maybe fifth?
The teacher always smiled at you.

You knew the answers,
so I copied off your paper,
then I mimicked the way you spoke
and held your head.
I even dressed like you.
Did you notice?

I've cheated ever since.
Now I can remember nothing,
none of the answers.
Even the questions slip away,
except for these:
Who am I? Where am I going?
What am I doing here?

TAKING BLAKE TO KANSAS

I showed William Blake the sunflowers
growing tall in the long grass of the prairie.
He admired them and explained to me
the sunflower weary of time in his poem was his own invention.

Blake wanted to visit the Garden of Eden and stroll through it naked
but settled for a drive through the Flint Hills.

When we came to Cawker City and stopped to buy gas,
we took a few moments to have our picture taken
beside the world's largest ball of siskal twine
(under the roof they built to keep it dry).

We waited our turn,
and Blake's breath came fast and ragged as he paced about.

Taking in the breadth of it, its height, its heft, its weight,
he wanted to know what the devil all that cord was binding,
what knots were used and how tight they were.

He made the tourists believe there was a figure pulsing inside,
its hide worn tender with the struggle,
a creature unable to breathe but sweating under all those layers,
worrying rude strings with horns and hooves and fingers.

Though he assured us only good would happen if the devil broke
  free,
We were all skeptical.
We dared each other, "Put your hands against the surface of the
  ball."

Suddenly, I couldn't wait
to feel it twitch under my palm.

HOW YOU BECAME THE BRIDE OF FRANKENSTEIN

First, like any girl, you had to invent yourself.
You had your nose shaved thinner.
You made them plump your lips.
You had your breasts done, twice.

All this before I could take you out
to dinner and a show.

Good thing—it gave me time
to learn how to use cutlery.

I was enraged
that you shrieked when you first saw my face.
You thought I was a monster.

Though I was crudely stitched together,
it had not occurred to me
I would have to court you.
No one had told me I would have to wait,
that the doctors would have to convince you
chicks dig scars.
Our first few dates were disasters.
When you would not hold my hand
I put my fist through a table.

When we disagreed
about what movie to go see
you tore the sleeve off my coat.

Can either of us say what made love happen?
We discovered we want to please each other.
We took a chance.
It helps that we have a lot in common.

No one else we know
started out with all their teeth and hair.

The noise we make
when we argue in public
frightens people. They run for their lives.
If, instead, they would turn and look at us,

they would see tears on our cheeks.
In no time, they would understand
what it took us weeks to learn ourselves:

we are children.

DURING THE TWENTIETH CENTURY

Poets who did not drink themselves to death
in colorful ways when they were young—
one tipped back too far on his stool
to get the last drop of beer in his glass
and, falling backwards, broke his neck—
killed themselves jumping off bridges
when they reached middle age.

In those days, they were hunted.
Most of the best lived in hiding.
Their poems were about absence.
Many were captured.
Imprisoned, they would scratch out lines
on walls, on the soles of their shoes,
on bars of soap.

Now they are no more doomed
or hunted than other folks.
But not everything has changed:
there is the poets' awareness
of the sensual, the work,
certain rituals
that have been passed down,
some since the days of Keats.

As soon as I wake up
each New Year's morning
I stumble to the bathroom
and fill the sink with cold water.
Dipping my finger in,
I write my name on the surface.

AFTER THE SUN SPLIT IN TWO

One half continuing east to west
Around the earth
While the other half began to orbit
From south to north,
We wasted years fighting
Over who was to blame.

Each sun has tried to outdo
The other in brightness.
Each has staked out
Its time in the sky,
So that, most of the time,
One can forget about the other.
When they meet, they glare.
Plants wilt. Roads melt.

Night has shrunk to an hour,
Too short a time
For stars to dominate.
While they can,
They blink and twinkle fiercely.

The moon, wooed by two suitors,
Turns pink
And becomes even more voluptuous.

She stays pregnant.
Her children speckle the sky.
They are all different sizes.
Some are grey. Some are gold.
Some are hues
We have yet to name.

Because we could count on them,
Clouds have become our gods.
Encouraged by worship,
They fill the air with music—
Continuous thunder.
We acknowledge
The rain and mud they bring as blessings.

Did I say
Since the split
There are twice as many colors?

Did I say
Sight has changed
So that everything stays visible?
Yes, more than that,
We hear every sigh, every mumble.
Flowers and herbs have proliferated
So there are new scents, new tastes.
Even touch is more than it was.

With no secrets,
We limit our definition of sin.

Who knew that would be so liberating?

SCHOOL

The last time I was in here my knees would fit under those desks.
Now I crouch to write along the top edge of the blackboard,
Pinching this nub until my knuckle whitens.

The knowledge gained here served me well
But my learning—like my body—is out of proportion.
I've stopped expecting my pinkie finger will grow to match the others.
I'm done with waiting for my lungs to expand
Down to the base of my ribs.
There's no hope my jaw will push forward
So my tongue can lie down comfortably.
Still, there's no reason for my education to remain stunted.

To learn something new I am letting go
Of something else, giving a voice to my doubts,
Searching for questions when none—at first—come to mind.

Shoulders hunched, I stare into the black.
My arms are tired from waving the eraser.
My eyes ache from watching the words rubbed gray,
disappearing.

Somewhere there's a stick of chalk long as my finger,
Maybe even a box of them,
But the truth is here, on the tip of this nub,
Where it scratches the surface.

BECAUSE I DID NOT THINK TO ASK

Five geldings, four mares
behind a barbed wire fence
in a field beside our school.

Knob-kneed, sway-backed.
Skin tight against ribs,
no shine to their coats.

They weren't what horses
were supposed to look like.
Every day on the bus
Rolling past them, it bothered me.

I wrote about those rackabones
in the student paper,
said they were mistreated, starving.

Soon they were moved
away from our classrooms.

A week later, the librarian
made a point of finding me,
and let me know
she had arranged to have them
settled in that little pasture.

They weren't neglected.
They were old.

She said they had seemed to like it
there, with the sun on their backs.

PAPER BIRD

The ticket came in the mail.
Mom opened the envelope
and left the snapshot of your license plate
face up on the table.
When you got home, Daddy,
I asked, "How did you come to run that light
way over on McGuire Street?"

You took the picture of your car,
and, bending one corner into the middle,
began to fold one section, then another,
pressing down with the side of your hand,
turning the paper over.

While you handled the paper you told us
"I saw a golden swan in flight—
her feathers flashing in the sun—
so beautiful I followed
up one street and down another
until I was lost."

Mom saw the holes in your story
but kept quiet, knowing
I needed your innocence,
Even of running a light.

Before the photo could take the shape of a bird,
the creases you made began to pucker.
The lines wore through.
I saw where it had torn.

It meant nothing when we sat at the table,
but, that night in a dream,
I could see through the slits in the paper
my Girl Scout leader standing naked
in front of a hotel mirror,
putting on lipstick.

THE SCHOOL AFTER SCHOOL

Most days my stomach starts hurting
as I take the long step down
from the bus,
before you come home,
when it is still possible
nothing will happen.
There is the sound
of your key in the lock.
There is setting the table,
then dinner.
If no milk is spilled
nothing will happen—
at least for a while—
but who can bear the waiting?
It isn't the belt,
not the blows against bruises,
the buckle on bone.

No. Not as much as you want to believe.
Nor the trouble with sitting down later.
You have taught me to flinch.
What scares me is thinking
that I'll learn to tremble.

MUSIC LESSON

On the piano bench,
That first day with Mrs. Whitehurst,
I heard her say, "First, sit up straight."

"Good. Put your hands up here."
She reached and grasped my knuckles,
Bending each slightly.

She pushed down a key
With the index finger of her right hand.
A tone rang out.

Mrs. Whitehurst said, "This is C."
She pointed to a dot on a page,
Off by itself, away from the lines.

So—I find each note
By starting at C
And counting up and down the keyboard.

G, it is time I learn your name
And the names of your brothers and sisters,
Time I learn to distinguish your voices
And where each of you sits at the table.

HOLDING PATTERN OVER TAMPA

The sky is not predictable.
Still, I never thought I would see
a seraph at this height
turning to glare at me,
crossing his arms
and twisting his neck around
to stare through the cabin window
of our jet.

The French fries I had in my bag—
dug out of the ground—
had damned me in his eyes.

By the same logic,
breast men are more spiritual
than leg men.
It is more exalted to die of pneumonia
than of colon cancer.

But who can argue with an angel—
especially at that speed,
especially in weather like that?

If I see him again,
what will I say?

If I remember to,
I will tell him that things on the ground
are not small like he thinks—
only far away.

I START MY LIFE AS AN OUTLAW

I

At first we thought he was joking,
The way he grinned as he proposed the thing,
But he did not join in our laughter.
Quickly, his baritone became more convincing
Than all our father's treble pieties.

This morning, at the stable,
Where my brothers and I waited
For our folks to finish their business,
It took no time for this man,
In his black suit with the scarlet vest,
To convince three farm boys—
Ready for anything that got us away from the fields—
Robbing the bank would be easy.

A matter of surprise.
A harmless threat.
Some fancy riding.

Tom said our mules would be too slow.
The man said,
"Then you should use horses."
Joe and I looked at each other.
We looked at the thoroughbreds in the stalls.

How excited we were
To weigh in our hands
The pistols he gave us!

The whole town knew what it meant
When we rode in with kerchiefs over our noses.
By the time we came out with the money,
The merchants had loaded their rifles.

I know these men.
They would have shot our mounts, tied us up,
And waited for the marshal,
But you can't expect a man
To shoot his own horse.
Tom and Joe didn't make it
To the end of the street.

II

This man and I ride those ponies lame
Then leave them by the creek
And plunge into the sea of grasses.

He jumps at the noise a jackrabbit makes.
I guess he expect wolves or buffalo.

He bends almost double to walk,
Though the grass is well above our heads.
He rubs his face
Where the side oats tickle him.

He pulled his pistol out
When a grasshopper landed on his shoulder.
He put it away when I said the posse
Might see the glint off the barrel.

Funny how the holes torn in the knees of his suit
Seem to bother him more than the bullet wound in his calf
The moaning wind has blown that pearl gray Stetson off
Eight times in the last hour.

III

If my brothers were alive,
I'd be laughing at him.

If Tom had lived,
We might have said the bank robber
Gave us unloaded guns to hold,
That he made us go with him.
Tom, people believed.

I recognize the L-shaped rock
With the sunflowers around it.
We are hard by the Curtis place.
When I get there,
I'll steal a horse and supplies.
First, I will have to shoot this fool.

Soon, the posse will set fires to drive us.

Before he realizes that I might do it,
Before I lose my nerve,
I'll ease my gun out.
Before they catch up with us,
Before we start to lose the light,
Before I smell smoke.

Now.

II

"Not all your light tongues talking aloud
Could be profound."

<small>ROBERT FROST</small>

CINDERELLA

No one has called me that for years!
Oh, don't worry, little girl.
You only want to know about the slipper.
As you can see, my feet are neither big nor small.
The truth is when the prince came around
the other girls would not trust their weight
to something that would break so easily.

Imagine being thin enough to dance in shoes of glass!
Well, I hardly ate at all back then. We were poor.
My step-sisters may have been full of themselves
but they had jobs, too. Gretchen took in laundry.
Beth was a seamstress.
Of course, what I did was more demeaning.
No one wants to be remembered as dirty
and I was black as the stove from hauling coal.
The heat of the furnace became like a mother to me,
melting sand I shaped into cups, into rings,
into that pair of transparent flats that made me famous.

Made to sit on the floor so the furniture wouldn't get sooty,
I wore rags, but I had stitched together a gown
From cast-off pieces of my step-sisters' clothes.
While they primped, I drew buckets of water for my bath.

Gray to my pores, I soaked, then I scrubbed myself pink.
At the ball, I looked rosy beside the pallid girls.

The rest of the credit goes to candlelight
by which moth-eaten scraps passed as lace.
The prince and I danced. We fell into a rhythm.
He held me close.

The scandal went beyond my genealogy.
Most people, in their hearts, believe
once you are soiled, you stay dirty.
That is why I have always been so fastidious.
Even I must remind myself
what separates me from you
—reeking as you bow before me
in your frayed and mud-dappled shift—
is mostly soap and water.

BOAR

When I ate so much bacon
my arteries grew stiff with white lard,
you sewed a pig's heart in my chest.
I woke to hear the grisly details of the operation.
Today, I dress to go home.
I rest my glasses on my snout,
put my cloven hooves in shoes,
pull on a leather coat.
In time, I may forget my flesh is pork.
But for now when people ask me questions
I open my mouth to answer
and listen for the squeal.

ALL THE BETTER

The restlessness
drove me outdoors.
A good thing, since now
I don't have hands
to turn a knob.

I headed for darkness
when the spasms started.
It wasn't
easy to find.

Thrown down
in wet leaves
I grew so hot
my muscles and bones
nearly melted.
When they grew soft,
they were able to shift
without snapping.

What was the worst part?
When my fingers pulled
back into my hands?
When my feet buckled?
When my nose and my jaw
thrust forward?

All of those
were so excruciating
I wasn't aware
when fur sprouted
or where my tail came from.

Afterwards, I didn't
have strength
to lick my poor
sore paws.

What sets me sniffing
at the crack of your door?

Hunger, sharp
as these teeth.

NOT WHAT YOU DREAMED OF, MOTHER, WHEN YOU CROSSED THE ROAD

Humpty Dumpty's last words

I can't see them
but I hear the soldiers talk.
They wonder what quantity
of French toast I might produce.

If I had the king's ear, I'd complain.

Not about the horses.
What could the horses do?
But the men—if they tried—
could put me together again.

They won't, though.
They think it is too late.

So they mill about.

More and more of my shell
gets stuck to the soles of their boots.

Any minute now, they will make coffee
and start dipping their bread in my yolk.

DISCRIMINATING PALATE

When your parents discovered
I could not tell
zinfandel from cabernet
they made a game of it.
Each night we go over,
what fun they have
laughing at me.

If I mispronounce something,
they pretend not to understand.

When you gather around the piano
before dinner is served
I am told to stay on the couch.
They say I can't carry a tune.

Perhaps there are other deficiencies
they have not bothered to point out.

I have been rendered mute.

When we sit for dinner
I remind myself
my tongue still has value.

It is a muscle I need
to push bread forward,
away from my throat,
up front to where my teeth can chew.

Without it,
I would choke.

OLD MAN RIVER'S AGITATION

Drops of rain that fall in this country
do not all join me.
Some are absorbed by the ground.
Some plop their way to the bottom of wells.
There are those that puddle and evaporate,
those drunk by roots,
those lapped by animals.
What runs to me I take to the ocean—
along with your sewage, your coal ash,
your chemicals, plastic, your boats.

I am a different creature
in different seasons.
When it is dry, I'm lethargic.
No one bathes in me
or wants a drink.
For a day or for a month
fish bob on my surface.
In the fall, leaves blanket me.
In winter, ice.

When storms come,
all that power changes me.
Whatever is caught in me drowns.

I fill basements, wash out roads.
When I recede, I leave a fat ribbon of muck.

Sweat may flow. Blood may pool.
Piss may drip on the cuffs of your trousers.
Tears may wear gullies down your cheeks
but what you cry will not match my wife—
the Missouri, or my kin the Amazon,
the Nile, the Ganges. . .
or even that creek half a mile from your house.

We are wetter than you,
more alive than the trickle of truth
you pretend not to know.

CHOU DYNASTY—
WHAT WE DO TO SAVE FACE

While lesser men run races
to see who is fastest
or take turns demonstrating feats of strength,
we noblemen make a contest
of growing out our nails.
It is a silly business.

Note how the index finger of this hand
and the middle finger make two chopsticks.
Perhaps the others—which are curved—
are different kinds of tools.
I wouldn't know.

It is so tiring to think of things I want
before I need them done
so I can issue orders,
so exhausting to watch my people
come and go rendering service
it would be easier to do myself.
Easier, except that I must move so slowly
to be sure a nail does not catch
on the fabric of my robe.

Why is it I have to scratch my nose with my knuckle?
Why must I sit motionless and be powdered
to cover a scratch on my cheek?

Do not be surprised if one day I command you
To trim them short
so I can grip a shovel or a broom if I desire.
Do not look shocked.
I will not turn peasant.

I only want to show you how a hole should be dug,
how a floor should be swept.

But who would I—what would I be with trimmed nails?
Not what I am. No. My equals would shun me.
Still, I am almost convinced
if it meant I would spend my days walking the roads
it would be worth it.

I imagine the pleasure of spinning an orange in my hands,
peeling it with my thumb.

HORSE SPEAKING TO RIDER

Because I am broken,
I let you nail on new iron
when shoes come loose from my hooves.

I don't fight when you back me into the trailer.
I eat your dry hay. I wait
too long for someone to muck out my stall.

Though it gags me,
I stand still when you put the bit in my mouth.

Because I am broken,
I let you bridle and saddle me.
I accept leather straps as part of me
as I accept you,
your weight shifting above me,
the reins pulling my neck right and left
or straight back to get me to stop.

As much as it scares me,
I go where you want.
I jump fences I am not sure I can clear.
I race and take the blame
if I am too slow
or if I stumble.

When I was wild
there was nothing to chase me,
to make me run like this.

Sweet is the apple you slice
and hold out on the flat of your palm.
And the way you take time to stroke my back and sides,
brushing me down, that, too, is sweet.
Best of all are your knees tight against me,
your heels in my flanks urging me on
as I gallop faster, faster, faster.

A TROPHY ELK SNIFFS THE AIR, THEN SPEAKS

Satisfying as it is
to clack antlers with another buck,
to drive him stumbling back on his haunches,
I have seen what one sharp point can do
to the side of a face, to an eye.

I've knocked my rack against branches,
running at full speed.
I have tangled it in vines
more often than I want to admit.

Impressive as it looks,
as attractive as it is to the does,
it is unwieldy,
a strain on my neck
when I have to bend down
to drink from a stream.
Balancing is difficult.
I stay thirsty.

When it was smaller and covered in velvet,
I felt princely,
and I couldn't wait for it to grow.
Now I look forward to shedding this burden.

I understand all of the reasons
why the devil's horns are short.

WHERE OUR WEIGHT MEETS THE WORLD

My grandfather's uncle traveled the globe
And left us bric-a-brac from everywhere.
He saw a woman in Hong Kong whose feet had been bound
And remembered hearing that Lucifer can change his shape
But his foot must stay the hoof of a goat.
So, at ten in the morning he was sure he had seen the Devil.

By noon he had seen many women taking tiny steps.
He asked why they walked that way.
He was told about the custom of binding.
In between, different women were Satan in disguise.
When he saw more than one together,
he believed in more than one devil,

And then he was sure it was something Lucifer had done,
So he could pass unsuspected through the world,
One of many who hobble.

SMALL TORMENTS

I only saw you when you raised a paw
To smite the flies around your nose.
The sight made me forget the tzizzing in my ear,
The bites, the anticipation,
The bumps, the indignity
Of slapping myself all the places mosquitoes were alighting. . .
The memory reminds me none are unmolested.
Deer have ticks; dogs have fleas,
And vise versa.
Even the eagle, whose loops take him over the sun,
Has mites crawling under his feathers
As he soars in and out of the clouds.

SALEM

When Abigail and Ann and Betty began to shriek with pain
and roll on the dirt floor
it was easy to believe that witches were behind it.

The maid admitted to signing the Devils' book.
The others—the three accused—claimed innocence,
but the girls would point and cut their eyes around,
crying, "She's pinching me! Make her stop!" We pitied them.

What those girls testified explained so much:
why a hen would stop laying, why a cow would go dry,
sick children, horses going lame.
All this was the work of the king of disorder,
who put spider webs in my way,
who hid my keys, who put a chair in my path to bark my shins,
whose servants don't use brooms for sweeping but for something
    else.
Here, Satan was exposed.

In front of the church one Sunday, Abigail pointed at my hat.
She said, "Look, a yellow bird!"
Others saw it too.
I plucked it off but saw nothing.
Maybe I heard the clap of wings.

Since then I've thought of little else but what kind of bird it was,
a mere canary or some demon riding me.
To this day my hat won't stay straight on my head.
Though I push it down tight
it's as if a bird nested there on the crown or perched on the brim.

I strain my eyes looking
for the place where the felt has been marred by the grip of its claws.
More than once, I've come close to pitching it into the fire.
Homes on this road stand empty, the houses of witches we hanged.
One, a woman I'd buy apples from, another, I once hired to mend
    my coat.
If all of the accused had gone to the gallows,
who would be plowing and planting these fields?
I doubt the ones who do that work fly through the air at night.
Nineteen swung by their necks and one we crushed with stones.

A DIFFERENT KIND OF WITCHCRAFT

She said she saw me fly across the moon.
She trembled, poor child, as she pointed her finger.

What bird or bat did she see that night?
What made her picture my face up there?

You'd think they had found wisps of cloud
in the straws of my broom.

Flying is what they would do if they could.
Not I. I have no interest in their heaven.

It suits me that instead of climbing stairs
to float in the breeze, a rope around my neck,

I am wearing weighted boots
and have been abandoned here in the woods.

Since I can't free my feet
and barely have the strength to shuffle,

they are sure I'll stumble, thirsty, to the creek,
sink in the mud and drown.

Come, Puss. I'll scratch your ears
and make you purr. You, I will tell the future.

Here, by this oak, I'll scratch out a hole we can drink from.
I'll catch you mice and tie their tails together.

You'll drag me what I need but cannot reach
until my legs grow stronger.

When I can lift them, I will hike, disguised,
over to where the Frenchmen live.

I'll turn my lead boots to gold once we get there,
And then chip off bits to sell a sliver at a time.

The reason I don't change them now:
gold would be heavier.

VOODOO

A soft toy began it:
a glorified pillow shaped like a bear cub, a bunny,
a kitten—which was it?—-something small that you loved,
that smelled like sleep.
As a toddler you were given
a plastic infant to hug to your chest.
Sometimes you would drag her by one leg.
Tilted, her eyes opened and closed.
Squeezed, she cried out.

After that, you received a small version of a grown-up girl.
Her feet were set on tiptoe for high heels.
She was someone to dress
and a way of imagining what you might do with your life.

Now, too old for bought images, you have made a strange doll
from your enemy's old clothes, some hair from her brush,
and a Polaroid picture.
You pinch her. You twist her cloth arms.
You stick her with pins.
You search kitchen drawers for your matches,
laugh at her—prone on the table.

BACK WHEN IT WAS POSSIBLE
TO SIPHON GAS FROM A CAR

When I was in high school,
I took a carton of milk from the kitchen
down to the street
and held it while a friend of mine
ran one end of a hose into a gas tank.
He sucked on the other end,
then retched and spat out gasoline.

He put the spewing end into the tank
of his green '67 Grand Am, reached for the carton
and rinsed and choked white foam on the asphalt.
He gulped down the rest of the half gallon.

Over time, things accumulate.
The pole in my closet sags
under the weight of shirts and pants.

Yesterday, I reached back and to the right
and took a blazer off a hanger.
I remembered I had worn it to a Kinks concert.
With a can of beer in each pocket,
I walked past the security guards in Hampton Coliseum
as they stopped all the girls and looked through their purses.

This morning, I spot a friend from
back in school in a coffee shop
and call out his name.
Limping, he comes to meet me. We sit.
He talks about the operation he will have on his hip
sometime next month.
I hold back from telling him any good news.
Leaving him, I laugh when I find myself
trotting from the coffee shop to the car.
Run, old legs, while you can.

THREE-LEGGED DOG

If the first tools were weapons,
the first trade prostitution,
the first art graffiti,
and the first song keening,
if the first religion was fear of cats,
the first dance was mock the cripple.

When to be human meant to run,
the damaged man who made a cane
was something strange,
something that poked along,
poking along with a stick that was sometimes
a shepherd's crook,
sometimes a spear.
When Moses threw it down,
it turned into a snake and crawled.

Picking it up, you lean on it, shift your weight.
May it help you to a place where whoring
Isn't a trade, where there is more to art
Than marking territory,
more to song than sorrow,
where faith and dance begin with stretching.
May that place be your home.

III

"It is enough, the freight should be
Proportioned to the groove."
EMILY DICKINSON

FLAG

It signifies nothing until it is raised
over the head of a breeze
while she holds her arms up,

nothing 'til it rests on her. I've watched a current smooth the cloth
down over her hips,
watched the skirt's slow dance.

I've heard an easterly moan and watched
as he wrapped a pennant shivering around himself
in the cold—looking for heat, for protection.

I've learned the material matters. Nylon's snap in the breeze is a
    protest;
A gust needs to breath.
A silk banner soothes. It is a formal garment. It flatters the shape.
Cotton's better for field work.

On hot days, I've seen sweat stick a flag to the wind
like a shirt to a man, seen the rise and fall
of it panting,

seen the fabric bag where the knees of the wind
stretched the cloth when he bent down.
I've seen flags hang, cast off, and wondered if the breezes died or
    just slipped off to sleep.

I've seen them tattered
and wondered what would stir the air up so against a country
that it would shred its banner, pull its buildings down.

I say she mourns, though I don't know who or what she has lost.
You would need fury to do this, to move beyond bluster, grab hold
    and let fly—
Rage and two strong hands.

The witnesses said she was grieving the old way.
All night they heard her keen.
Out one window, she rolled in ashes.
Out another, she tore at her clothes.

CRAWLING OR FLOATING,
I CAST SHADOWS

You think this is easy—
try it, but first, take my burden of water.
You won't stay in the blue very long.

I watch how you walk, your head high,
swinging your arms, your palms empty.
What does it matter where you go?

Winds push and pull.
Lightning tears holes in me.

Jets slice through, leaving smoke in my wounds,
When I stretch out, I feel the bruises you see on my flanks.

I'll surrender my treasure,
but first I'll make you wait 'til your crops are brown and brittle,
until you are thirsty enough,
then I'll let it fall through my fingers a drop at a time.

IN KINDRA'S HIVE

For Kinda McDonald

This heaven's a storehouse of sweetness
packed into cells, more golden than gold.
I am a drone
and the angels are worker bees. Some come and go,
fling down to the fields, to the flowers out in the bright sun
to get nectar, while others stay in the apiary
and their transparent wings churn the air to keep it cool,
to keep the names written in wax
and the walls themselves from melting.
The buzzing is praise, praise for the Queen, for the Goddess.
I pretend it is for me.

A SONG INSTEAD OF SPEECH

I am no smarter than I was as a man
but I know things—the rigor of flight,
the view from the clouds
with eyes sharper than my beak,
what it is to land on a branch
and have it sway under my weight.

How can I explain how I know
the distance between my wing
and the wings of the other sparrows
when we fly?

How can I explain how I know
where you are every moment,
my bride, my soul?

My life is concentrated
by being so small—the size of the fist
in which you hold your car keys.

From my perch in the pecan tree
on the side of the hill,
I watch you limp down the stairs
on your way to where the Buick's parked
across the street.

I raise my voice and sing
a tune we used to sing together.

Slowing down and then stopping
by the crack in the sidewalk,
*y*ou turn and listen.

Shifting your feet,
you lift your chin;
pursing your lips, you whistle the chorus—
those notes are the air that I breath.

If you'd cup your hands.
I would swoop down
and land in that nest.

CUT ME LOOSE

The crows remember—though you don't—
when I could clap my hands and give chase,
howling and waving my arms.

This was when I came inside at night,
when I wore my own clothes.

How long has it been since I've bothered
to wipe my nose on your sleeves?

Cataracts block my vision.
I am deaf from the cawing.

Every night, I am soaked with dew,
Every day, I bake in the sun.
Ticks crawl all over me.

Season in, season out, I tell myself:
you feel nothing.

Driving past, it disturbs you
to see me bent double in the field.

Pulling over, you park by the ditch;
You get out and push your way through the corn,
coming to tighten the ropes
that must stand me upright.

How stunned you are
when you start to square my shoulders
and my flesh twitches under your fingers.
How you jump at my groaning!
You can feel my breath on your face.

What can I say when you ask me,
"Uncle, how long has it been?"

YANKED OUT OF THE HOUSE ON A ROPE

My nose is no longer a smudge on my muzzle;
it's every hollow and passage, every thick and thin bone
in my damp little skull.
I sniff
and I gather the scent of a scrap of bread by the curb
alongside the fidgety smell of the squirrel on the trunk of the maple,
and the birds in its branches,
and the birds that were there yesterday.
I smell the trees and the grass and the dust
and the old carpet rolled up on the porch of the house across the
    street.
I know twelve kinds of smoke and six kinds of wool,
cottons, brands of gasoline.
I know things you will never understand—
not until your nose is opened.

Fill your lungs; the odors are telling a cycle of stories.
The dogs have left me their boasts, their grievances.
I know all the creatures—their names, where they live,
their sex, their diseases.
I prefer the unwashed to the perfumed.
I know who you have been with and what you're afraid of.
You can hide nothing from me.
Now that I've found what I want and have buried my face in the
    grass,
you can't pull me away.

A TOURIST IN THE LAND OF KARMA

Yogi Shamalyan, there is beauty in this vibrant smoke,
layered yellow, red, brown, from earth to sky,
but it makes my lungs burn.

Here in Delhi, I shower twice a day,
apply sunscreen hourly,
eat, drink, avoid the sun.
These take up time.

Still, yesterday I made it to the India Gate,
took a guided tour of the Presidential Palace,
and measured the shadows
on your famous sundials
between trips to the latrine.

This morning you have given me a mat
and a place to sit in the shade.
You taught me how to fold my legs
and told me to focus on my breathing.

How do I close my ears
to the sounds of traffic and the melodies
of so many languages I don't speak?
Diesel, mildew, cow dung mingle
And make me cough.

Back home, the fragrance of cut grass
will fill my nose—that is, once I do the mowing.
Right now, I imagine Ed, my neighbor,
on his porch, looking over at my overgrown lawn.
He wonders where the hell I have gone to.

"Concentrate." You tell me.
"Inhale. Exhale. Inhale."

How needy I am,
every minute of the day.

SINCE NO BROKEN THING CAN BE HOLY

The tablets that Moses threw down,
the testimony of the Almighty,
were left at the foot of the mountain.
With no reason to clear them away, rock among rocks.
They remained there for children to piece together and read.

Sometimes they would shift the parts back and forth
to make them say different things.
Someone would notice the marks on the back of a piece
and they would turn them all over
and read what was written there;
in time, they would turn them again
and rediscover what they had once thought was the front.

Some parts would have only one word,
meaningless by itself,
others having words enough to be part of the truth
that might pass for truth.

Sometimes a bit would go missing and turn up
as the point of a spear
or in a ring of rocks around a fire.
When it was time to leave that place
the stones became souvenirs.

From father to son, mother to daughter,
they were passed down,
until now I have this rock
my grandfather used to prop open the door to his study,
a rock I would pick up as a boy and turn over and over,
wonderng why the letters had not worn away.

BLACK HAT

So many skies,
more skies than there are hats
and more eccentric shapes
and varied sizes,
each fez and each fedora made to suit a particular sky.
The different skies are different colors,
different shades of colors,
but none of them is black.
Let me be fooled
but I am not fooled in this.
Whether the stars are moths or holes the moths have eaten
in the crown of heaven's felt,
the moths I have caught in the morning
are stained around the mouth,
blue or pink, orange, silver-gray,
but none would match the darkness of your shuttered room
or share the polished hue inside your heart.

THE SEAM WHERE SPIRIT
AND FLESH ARE JOINED

You see this—
Along the crotch where the cloth is torn a little?

I pray for a needle and thread
Or the strength to tear the two pieces asunder.

People say, "When they separate, the spirit will fly."
But you hear all kinds of foolishness.

I bet, at most, it will hop like one leg
That's set free of the other.

In time, the seam will fray, the cloth will come apart
And I will know for sure.

Until then, I have a hole in the seat of my pants
Where the wind blows.

THE SHAPE CHANGER'S APOLOGY

For Gayle

It is hard for you,
not knowing when I might change
into a river, an elk, a stone.

I am so grateful you put up with it.
It awes me how faithful you are,
sharing your bed when it means
you are lapped by my waters,
when it means you are rubbed by my horns,
not knowing when I will return
to my human form.

Wary as my many creature-selves are,
you tame them all.

Most of all, I thank you for those days
you raised me up the flagpole
so I could flap, terrified, in the wind,
and lowered me down as dusk neared,
gathering me in your arms.

MONKEY

Because you are little
you hide better than anyone,
and when you are tired, you're carried;
but a child's fascination with dolls or toy soldiers
is about being big.
Growing means half the time your clothes don't fit,
You hit your head on the bottom of the table,
Your mother expects more of you.
Eventually a cup becomes safe in your hands.
More and more you are able to reach things;
still, for some things you will have to climb.
It's hard to watch you scramble
when it's so easy to imagine you tumbling.
This breed of monkey scales trees
and climbs mountains so tall we have to carry air
to breathe. We who reach heights
hand over hand or a step at a time
dream of flight. We wake knowing the dream of flying
and the dream of falling are the same.
On your way up you will lose your footing.
Your hand will slip.
Know that some limp for days, some for life.
Most find an attitude that pleases them
or simply doesn't frighten them.

If you reach the top, rest a while,
let the wind blow in your face,
and then start looking for the best way down.

PRATTLE

Having made promises,
who has not cursed his own tongue,
thinking: soft as you are,
you have caused so much trouble,
lying and boasting and telling the uneasy truth?
You that I feed as much as my belly,
you razor, you honeyed and silken
but slippery, twisted, forked tongue,
I have bitten you two thousand times
when I'd rather have leashed you.
Soft as you are,
why do you rise from your crib
to strike my irregular teeth?
You lick my chapped lips and I worry.
When I open my mouth, people stare.
They are wondering
what will come out of that darkness.

THE SEEDS OF THE PEPPER

Speaking about emotion
We speak of the heart.
But it is another muscle
I think of,
One less constant,
Made to take extremes
Of temperature,
A muscle with receptors
In its tip for sweetness
While those that take in bitterness
Are closer to the throat.

The same way sourness
Is recognized only by certain buds
Along the side of the tongue,
My heart has places
That feel nothing but outrage.

The appetite for flavor
And the appetite for emotion
Are greater than the belly's need.
We crave something new, something exotic,
And we want more and more of the same.

What I desire (I swear)
Is to let go of my anger,
To clean my heart's palette
So I can feel other things:
Tenderness, pity,
Triumph, even fear and sorrow.
What I want is to prepare myself
To taste peace, to engender love.

DREAM ON

When wealth and fat were synonymous
and our bones stuck out at crazy angles,
each of us wanted to be the man who took up the most room,
the one whose cheeks crowded his vision.

Before we understood affection,
we thought the man with the most wives
was someone to envy, a man rich in love.

To be famous means that people are tired of you
before you met them.

The man of property spends all his time mowing grass
Or else feeling cheated by whoever does his chores,
yet we want the burden of choosing which car to drive,
of rooting around in a drawer full of keys.

The handsome man's heart beats faster when voices are raised.
When there is ice on the sidewalk he clinches his jaw,
imagining his face with a flattened nose.

Better to envy the man rich in years.
His memories are more real than his gnarled fingers.
His skin loose enough his smiles come easily.
His very hair is silver.

THE VOICE OF THE GRASS

Let me make a deal with you.
Admit you're exhausted from mowing and watering,
edging and raking,
putting down seed, herbicide, fertilizer.

I'll confess I am sick of the din of your machines,
of your meddling, of each blade being even.

Let me stray into flowerbeds,
spill onto sidewalks.
Let my leaves grow until they hang down.

Let my land turn to field,
making room for the chickweed, the clover,
for crickets, beetles, mice, and snakes.

Let my seeds shake loose.
Let them scatter. Let all kinds of seedlings take root.
Leave the saplings to grow.

Expand your kitchen and redo your bath.
Paint. Tile. Redecorate.

Better yet, let clothes be your symbol of order.
Have them tailored and cleaned, starched and ironed.
Shine your shoes. Shoot your cuffs. Comb your hair.

IV

"I cried for bread a careless world
Pressed to my lips a stone."

FRANCES ELLEN WATKINS HARPER

BETRAYAL MAKES A BETTER STORY

With thanks to Chris Joyner

First, put on clothes
you do not care about getting dirty.
Wear shoes that won't pinch your feet
when you cut across your lawn
to shake hands with your new neighbor.

Next, recognize the shape of your nose,
the color of your eyes, your heritage—
most of the things you take pride in
are not accomplishments.

It will not happen all at once.
You will have to learn
to listen to people you've dismissed,
to believe the truth
of what the cell phone cameras show.

Changing you mind will have a cost.
Old friends will turn against you.
Jokes that make you laugh
will no longer be funny.

Are you prepared
for your heart to open?
Are you ready
for all those red petals to uncurl?

THIRTY MILES NORTH OF THE BORDER

I came here when I married Fred.
I was too shy to talk to farmhands.
As long as my husband spoke their lingo,
we did fine.
Our kids, of course, got it at school.
I used to have them complain for me
if mud was tracked in the kitchen
when I was making lunch for everyone
or if they laughed too loudly at the table.

The kids grew up and moved away.
Fred died. I sold the farm but kept the house.
I love the quiet
and the view of the hills out the window.

The other day I went shopping and I ran into Ruth.
No one else that I know still lives around here.
She told me all about her kids and grandkids.
She asked how Sonny's doing
and how Sue likes her new job.
What was I supposed to say?
That I don't hear from them
since they gave up on my moving?
I'm not a city gal. I don't even get to town that often.

I talked about my quilting,
how I am raising two new breeds of chicken,
how I am finally learning to speak Spanish
using one of Sonny's old school books.
I said I've been writing songs.
When I offered to sing some for her
she moved on pretty quickly.

I guess I can't really say I am learning Spanish
after what happened this morning.
A Mexican boy knocked on my back door.
He wanted to mow my yard.
I took the opportunity to use what I had taught myself
to barter with him.
At first I spoke slowly, then loudly.
After a while, I realized he was embarrassed for me.
It seems I have invented a new language
only I understand.

THE IDEA OF ORDER VACATIONS
IN KEY WEST

After Wallace Stevens

Not how long was she here,
How much did she drink
Before she started singing?

Hush! It was a single tumbler of sangria
With dinner at El Meson de Pepe.

In the chorus,
The conchs were shaking maracas
And singing along.

As a tourist,
She could see things fresh,
Look at the palms and discern
A different intelligence, a different God,
Inventing trees without the thought of branching—
No boughs, no twigs,
Instead, gigantic leaves.

A richness not of her design:
New plants, new birds,
Side by side with the almost familiar.

This is the ocean,
Only here it is bottle green.

Clap your hands to rouse the roosters.
Set them crowing.

Fill your lungs with the sweetness

Of the island flowers—orchids, hibiscus. . ..

Sing louder, Goddess.
Sing and shake your hips.

MY ALCATRAZ

I pulled a button off my shirt,
balanced it on the back of my thumb.
I flipped it,
then got down on my hands and knees.
I felt around in my cell
'til I found it.

Now this is what I do.

Sometimes it lands on the bunk,
sometimes in the sink,
but mostly down here on the floor.
I find it,
then stand up and flip it again.

From the Hole, I can hear metal doors
bang open, clang shut.
It reminds me of sunshine,
gulls, voices,
the view of the bay I once had
and the city,
so close I could smell the bread baking.

I have darkness, numb fingers, cramped toes.
My knees ache when I stand or bend down.
They ache twice as much now, pressed against the cold floor.

There's a button here, somewhere.

THIS ONE MADE OF RUBBER

Is supposed to help you breathe underwater.
This moves the air around.
Push the button; see the blades whirl.
This thing—all wire and springs—
Is a trap to catch rats.
Watch! Don't let it get your thumb.

Told a poem's a little machine,
I didn't believe it, not until I took one apart
And looked at the gears,
Not 'til the oil from its chain was on my fingers.

I'm not sure what possessed me to climb aboard this one.
Noisy, hard to steer, but it eats up the road.
When I pulled to a stop and turned it off,
As I swung my leg over and balanced myself
In that quiet,
I realized how hard my heart was beating.

I WAS TOLD WHAT I FELT

was weakness leaving my body,
told that strength or resolve or, failing those, wisdom
would take its place.
I learned other things could fill that space.

I believe you now when you say
we have more foreign cells than human cells in our bodies.
Inside, I am all viruses and hurts.
Some mornings, I have more fear in me than spirit.
Some nights, distress fills what was empty in me,
aches and misgivings,
but even those mornings, those nights,
pain is weakness leaving my body.

Every morning I feel more powerful.
Every night I know more secrets.
I prick the ball of my thumb.
I stick again, this time hard, and I ask myself,
"Is there more blood in this finger than pain?"

RAPUNZEL'S REAL HUSBAND

When I stooped through the window
and entered the dark tower,
I wasn't the first boy to call your name
and walk up that stone wall,
fingers tangled in your locks.

The prince who came before me
was too eager to leave someone who clung so close
for the warmth of his body.
Scrambling out, he fell
and blinded himself on a thorn bush.

Blue lipped, shivering girl!
Dressed in a summer frock
with no coat or quilt or blanket
to fashion into rope for you to shimmy down.

Pretty as you were,
like him, I knew your grip on me
was not affection.

When I went to leave,
you wanted to know
what my coat was made of,
how bread grows, how fish make their way
across the ground.

These questions made me laugh,
and then you didn't believe what I told you.

I came back, dragging a ladder I borrowed
from my father's barn,
through half-melted, smoke-colored snow,
across broad fields, bumping over roots in the woods.

Like everything else,
the ladder was new to you.
I said, "Pile your hair up on your head.
Turn around. Step on the rungs."

The witch who had imprisoned you
found the tracks the ladder left
too obvious to follow; she was sure
it was a trap.

I can't recall what I did last week
or the date of our anniversary
but each time you smile
I remember the triumphant grin you showed me
when your feet touched the ground.

BAGGAGE

If you were a dog, you would carry your bone in your mouth.
You would pee on everything to claim it,
Bark and growl to defend what's yours.
But you are human. You have pots and jars and cans
To store things, locks and alarms on the doors.
Morality, weapons, and laws protect your possessions.

Somewhere men strap bags on donkeys to start a journey.
As they travel on foot through heat and cold, rain and snow,
They sling packs on and off. They zip and unzip,
Buckle and unbuckle, button and unbutton again.
They grip the straps, run a finger over the seams.
And in train stations, bus depots, airports,
A bag is lifted and set down again, nudged with a foot,
And then clutched on a lap.

Some people can balance jugs on their heads
And walk for miles. I can't keep a wheelbarrow from tilting.
On a shorter journey, a boy totes a pail,
A woman lifts a baby, a man juggles groceries,
A girl swings a purse.

The clothes you are wearing don't weigh enough to bother you,
But you can feel what's in your pockets: keys,
A wallet, maybe a knife or hard candy or a lucky rock,
But nothing more valuable than your hands,
That bring everything to you,
That grab, caress, manipulate,
That must, sooner or later, let go.

THE FISH GATE

In the walled cities, every gate had a name
that told you what went out or came in.
They were places of meeting and judgment.

If each door you passed through were recognized—
from the glass one at the grocery that opens at your approach
to the crimped tin one on the shed held shut with string—
would it help you be more in the moment?

Yes, front doors and back doors,
cupboards ,anything with a hinge,
even the curtain on your shower.

This is a gate.
You've spent years preparing to pass between these walls.
The tassel moves from one side to the other
and you are out in the wind and the sun.
God bless your exits and your entrances.

ANIMAL TALK

The fox's word for speech is salesmanship,
While the sheep call it complaint.
Bees hum so they will know when they're content
And when they're angry.
Snakes tell each other there are two forms of language:
Lies and self-deception,
While the bear tells her cubs
They have three reasons to open their mouths—
to threaten, to boast, and to eat.
The mockingbird you know about, and the owl.
Dogs bark, growl, beg, and one of those they got from us.
Given time, you will remember which animals taught you
To chatter, to whine, to rant.
What will teach you to listen?

DADDY LONG ARMS

Back in my hometown, there's a man
(he is old now.)
who would not let go of the coffin
in which his wife lay.
They finally took him by the arms
and moved him back a little.
They thought they had him clear
but when they dropped the lid
it took off the tips of his fingers.
No one knew 'til she was buried.
His cry of pain was a cry of grief.
No one would look at him
with his balled up fists.
No one saw the blood.
As a boy I would watch him
out of the corner of my eye,
pushing his change to the edge
of the store counter with his palm.
As children, we'd speculate
how long his fingernails grew
in the land of the dead.
We were certain that he could reach out
and bring small things back to life—
birds, houseplants, guinea pigs—
and find anything that was lost
that would fit in his hands.

YOU SAY DISTANCE MEANS NOTHING

Airplanes, automobiles, telephones, television and telescopes,
They mean we can see everything,
Reach out and put our fingers in any hole in the world.
And I say, "At a price."

Spice and disease know no boundaries.
Ideas go begging in every borough and village in the world—
Begging money for shoes, bicycles, cab fare, for passage
To the next shore.

Everything's portable—whole planets, whole galaxies.
And I say, "The world where you find everything
Is the world where you escape nothing."

I tell you, "As current travels down the line,
The wire drags back a bit of the power."
What I mean to say
Is that I'll miss you in New York,
Even for three days, even with talking on the phone.

Now that everything's close but you're far away,
I miss your touch and the taste of your kiss.
When I come home, I'll bring bagels,
And photographs of Central Park,
And stories of how dangerous Manhattan was
When I went there alone.

THE NIGHT CRAWLER'S QUESTIONS

You try to push me on your hook,
And I wrap myself
around your finger.
My tenderness bothers you
more than my wiggle.

Until your pinch,
the grit and flake and rot
of the world
traveled through my gut
as I mixed marl and clay,
silt and manure,
leaf mold and sand.

It was my privilege
to loosen the path of the roots.

You can't expect me to lie still
while you prick your thumb,
impatient to cast me in water.

Why would you do this
when you could use a lure?

Wanting a tug on your line
and fish for dinner,
have you forgotten
all your food depends on me?
Do you love anything
the way that I love the soil?

Without the work I do,
no green will take hold
of this dirt you are so
contemptuous of,
that you wipe off your hands.

WE SHARE THE WORLD

Flies crawl on the meat
   where the butcher hacks
and you show it   Jacob Lawrence

while my legs are stuck in the paint on your canvas
and my wings beat
      working to free me
              I see this market around us
and I see the way you make it flat
        filling your picture
            with orange
blue   red   black   with booths that stretch to the ocean
   people here to buy
        cloth   rugs   baskets
you show us swarming   we're dots

   now I've freed myself from your painting
     I freckle the skin of the people
with my feet
   specks of orange

where I light on their arms, on their necks
      my friends halo the heads of people
who stroll, who dodge   chicken   children dogs
   their sandals stepping
    around   puddles   caca

                              thick in the air
we swarm what is damp   what is warm what is sticky we're on the
    melon
                 the fish now we're   on the bowl of the man in front
       of your easel
                          he lifts the spoon to his mouth
we land on his cheek   we buzz in his ears

THREAD TO NEEDLE

It does no good to say
the knot that binds us together
is made of my body

or that I'm the one who will live
in the fabric, mending the tear,
holding the button on.

Each of us is useless without the other.
You, all shiny thin steel,
push my loops through, pull me tight.

The joy you have in piercing
has a purpose beyond making holes.
You've made me useful.

Your eye showed me where I was needed.
Blind, I had told myself
I was content on the spool.

WHERE WAS I GOING?

When I ran out of gas
and had to trudge down the highway
in the freezing downpour with no coat—
When I ran over a collie
and went door to door
'til I found the dog's owner—

When my brakes gave out
going down the mountain—
skidding, accelerating—
finally jolting off the road,
ending up axle deep in a muddy field—
how long did I wait,
stroking the grooves on my keys,
for a tow truck?

When I cut that guy off
and he followed me, honking his horn;
when he screamed out his window he'd kill me—
Not able to get away from him,
afraid to go home,
I pulled into the parking lot
of a police station,
and he peeled away.

How long did it take
    for me to feel safe again,
to stop checking my mirrors
    for his red Camaro?

When I hit the deer
    and she came through my windshield,
those sharp hooves first,
    did I feel lucky
when I pushed open the door
    and climbed out?

When I noticed four cars in a ditch
    and slowed down
but still spun around on black ice
    until I faced the traffic—

When I picked up the phone
    and was told my best friend had been killed;
when I sobbed and my shoulders
    shook so much
the steering wheel twitched as I drove—

Why was I in such a hurry,
    when I got my second speeding ticket
within 24 hours.

When I unwrapped a BLT
   and bit into it,
mayonnaise dripped on my pants—
   I fumbled to blot it from where it landed
and weaved into the next lane.
   How is it I did that and lived?

When the yellow Beetle in front of me
   lurched to a stop
and I rammed into the back of it,
   and the truck behind plowed into
my bumper, and then it was four cars, five, six
   that had to be pulled apart—

When metal shards in the street
   shredded my two front tires;
when my car stalled in an intersection
   and I was T-boned;

when the puddle I drove through
   was so deep it ruined my engine
and water glugged in
   through a hole by the brake pedal
and soaked my shoes, my pants—
   Did I blame myself?
Was I partly to blame?

When the driver of the black SUV
   coming toward me was drunk;
when the driver behind me
   nodded off and slumped forward;

When my van caught fire
    and, standing back from the heat
by the guardrail, I watched the flames
    lick the white paint black,
as traffic blew past me,
    I didn't think about what was burning,
what I'd lost.

No. I was wondering
    what vehicle I would be driving next,
what make, model, color,
    how long I would have to wait
for something to bring me here, home,
    where I'd kick my shoes off,
drop my keys in the bowl by the door.

www.ingramcontent.com/pod-product-compliance
Lightning Source LLC
LaVergne TN
LVHW051647080426

835511LV00016B/2543